The Race

Debbie Croft

Photographs by Lindsay Edwards

Contents

Race Day at School

Mom and Dad and Tom came to my school today. They came to see me run in a race.

My Shoes

I had my blue **shoes** on for the race.

The Race

Milly and Kate
went in my race.

We went up to the **line**.
The teacher said, "Go!"

I ran fast.

Milly and Kate
ran fast, too.

We ran up
to some trees.

We ran back
to the teacher.

I won the race.

After the Race

I looked for Mom
and Dad and Tom.

They looked for me.

I liked running
in the race.

Glossary

line

shoes